TRAMS PICTORIAL

C000214425

The year 2004 is a significant one for the Blackpool Tramway. It was 70 years ago when the first Open 'Balloon' car made that 17 mile journey from the English Electric factory in Preston to the seaside tov start of a major transformation in the town's transport system. Of the men who designed, built and delivered these tramcars back in the 1930s, who would have ever imagined that a large number of them would still be in service in the next century, still running along the same promenade and still doing exactly what they were designed to do all those years ago.

Like many public transport systems in Britain today, the Blackpool Tramway has its problems and compared to how it used be, it's a very different system today. Likewise, Blackpool as a town has changed and the once millions of summer visitors has declined virtually year on year but through it all, every springtime, those magnificent creatures emerge from winter hibernation and grace that promenade once more. How lucky we are. How grateful we all should be and how honoured we are today to celebrate 70 years of the Streamlined fleet.

Over the next 50 pages, this book takes you on a roller coaster ride around the Blackpool tramway and its tramcars. From the golden days of the 1950s, through to the OMOs in the 1970s, all-over advertising in the 1990s and the modern bright liveries on the Twin cars today. This tramway has it all and this book contains a very small piece of it.

It's an old cliché, but I hope you get as much pleasure from viewing this book as I did compiling it. Many thanks to Tony Wilson of Travel Lens Photographic and to John Bromley for access to his superb collection of tram slides. The biggest thank you of all though must go to Walter Luff whose forward thinking and truly inspirational design of electric tramcars more than 70 years ago made the Blackpool fleet what it was then and what it is today. A remarkable man by any standards.

Thanks are also extended to Elizabeth, Mary and Jason.

Enjoy the book.

Nick Meskell

July 2004

Opposite: As part of the 70th anniversary celebrations in 2004, popular Railcoach 679 was painted into the 1980s livery. Stirring up the sand in the grooved rail, 679 passes Central Pier on 12th April 2004. (NM)

Front cover: Back in the summer of 1975, all-over advertising on the tram fleet was introduced on two advert cars. Balloon 707 advertised 'Empire Football Pools' while Brush car 622 was the 'Tigerrific' tram, advertising Blackpool Zoo. Three decades and hundreds of designs later, 622 is still remembered as one of the best of all time. The tram is seen at Pleasure Beach inner loop waiting out time before a Little Bispham journey. (JB)

First Published 2004

ISBN 0-9548035-0-7

Published by **Train Crazy Publishing**,
PO Box 13, South Shore, Blackpool. FY4 1TA.
Telephone and Fax: 01253 346005
Email: admin@tram-trainvideos.co.uk
Website: www.tram-trainvideos.co.uk

Printed in England.

OPEN BOATS

Above: 'Blackpool - Always Welcome' reads the roadway arch at the southern end of the tramway, near Starr Gate. The Boat car in the picture is interesting for its swivel head trolley which would have allowed it to run around the Marton route, and note the four strings of lights from the tower. It is not possible to make out the fleet number but the photo dates back to the 1958-1962 period. (JB)

Opposite: Car 236 was the last of the 12 Boat cars built in 1934 and today, numbered 607, it is one of just five surviving Boat cars in Blackpool. The photo shows 607 on the drop from the main promenade to the tram stop at Gynn Square. 607 is in typical late-1980s condition with original windscreens and gold fleet numbers. (JB)

BIRTHDAY GIRLS

Looking smart in the 1930s livery, complete with trolley arm and black and white destination blinds, 'PRINCESS ALICE', 706, stands at Fleetwood Ferry on 2nd May 2004. Having survived the 1980 collision with 705 and dodged the scrap man, this tram is pride of the fleet today. (NM)

For 2004 a green and cream livery from every era will be represented on the Balloon cars and this is one of them, car 712 in the 1960s-style. The repaint was kindly sponsored by TRAMS Magazine, and complete with black and white destination blinds and Corporation crests, 712 certainly looks the part. The tram is at Cocker Street on 31st May 2004. (NM)

WITHDRAWN BALLOONS

Above: Although 2004 is very much a year for celebration, a number of the Balloon fleet will not run during the year having been withdrawn from service or because they are undergoing major overhauls. Car 713 is one of the lucky ones and at the time of writing is undergoing a 'heritage' overhaul. The photo above is another typical 1980s scene with 713 in the 1980s livery loading up next to the long gone northbound waiting shelter at Talbot Square. (JB)

Opposite: It was just another photograph, on a typical day at Pleasure Beach on 12th October 2001 as 704 entered the outer loop with 715 on the inner loop and, just in view, 717. You wouldn't have looked twice at a photo like this but just three years on, it's already a huge piece of history, following the withdrawal from service of all three cars in spring 2004. Thankfully, 715 was reinstated but 704 and 717 will never see the light of day again unless they receive major overhauls. (716 was also withdrawn). (NM)

TAKE A TRIP INTO THE WONDERFUL WORLD OF 'LITTLE ITALY' IN BLACKPOOL FOR YOUR QUALITY GIFTS!

LITTLE ITALY THE GREATEST SHOW ON EARTH!

ORIENTAL CHINA · FURNITURE · PAINTINGS
CAPO·DI·MONTE · PORCELAIN · CRYSTAL
& GENUINE VENETIAN GLASS DIRECT FROM ITALY

CATCH A TRAM

PLEASURE BEACH

LITTLE ITALY
NORTH PIER · BANK HEY ST.
UNDER THE TOWER
PROM · CHURCH STREET
FRONT & REAR CORAL ISLAND
CENTRAL DRIVE
GOLDEN MILE CENTRE

WIN A HOLIDAY TO ITALY AT ANY ONE OF THESE CENTRES

GENUINE
20th CENTURY
CAPO DI MONTE

LITTLE ITALY

719

1980's ADVERT BALLOONS

Above: Following on from 622 and 707 in 1975, and 634 in 1976, car 719 became Blackpool's fourth all-over advert tram in 1981. Taken about 20 years earlier in exactly the same location as the previous photo, this is 719 in its advert livery, a pleasing design for 'Little Italy' which was carried from March 1984 to May 1987. Today, of course, 719 is the 'Walls Ice Cream' tram and barely resembles the vehicle above. 719 and 712 were the first two Balloons to run with pantographs. 719 was fitted out in May 1985. (JB)

Opposite: The emergence in Blackpool of the fast food chain McDonalds in the 1980s prompted the company to advertise on a tram car and 718 was chosen. This was the first of two such designs for McDonalds and this one was carried from April 1988. Today of course, 718 is a Millennium car. The photo is taken on North Albert Street in Fleetwood. (JB)

GREEN TWINS

From all cream in the 1960s through to half green/half cream in the 1980s, the Twin cars were always in the shadows and always second best to the Balloons. Both of these photos show how bad things had become in the late 1980s with body panel dents, chipped and damaged paintwork, rust and a general absence of TLC. Both sets still carry gold fleet numbers and the Blackpool Transport logo which was crudely glued onto the body sides post-deregulation in 1986. 682+672 are at Broadwater. 687+677 are about to pass under the section breaker at Rossall School. (JB)

TWIN CAR DAWN

Above: Although repainted and fitted with pantographs in the early 1990s, Twin car life remained virtually static and would probably still be that way had it not been for the events of Thursday 17th October 2002. Due to the condition of the track, double deckers were banned from running between Thornton Gate and Fleetwood and with no other option, the Twin car rose like a phoenix and saved the day. The photo above is a small piece of history, taken at Cleveleys at 06.25 on Friday 18th October after 683+673 had just reversed on the crossover prior to working the 06.29 Cleveleys to Starr Gate. Not only was this the first time that Twin cars (all seven sets) had been used on the timetabled Fleetwood service, it was also the first time a Twin car had turned at Cleveleys on a scheduled service. (NM)

Opposite: With the double decker ban set to last throughout 2003, there was no option but to use Twin cars on the Fleetwood service. During the winter/spring 2002/2003 period a start was made on refurbishing these sets and by late summer 2003, four of them had passed through the workshops. In addition to repaints, the trams were also fitted with saloon heaters and latterly, improved head and tail lights. The photo opposite shows a remarkable line up of Twins 'on shed' on Monday 31st May 2004. (NM)

Opposite: Why paint them in green and cream when you can paint them like the colourful Metro liveried buses? That suggestion was probably mooted sometime late-2002 and the result is four Twin sets in four different colour schemes. This is 681+671 in the Line 2 light green and yellow livery. The trams are seen near Cabin on driver training duties on 22nd April 2004. (NM)

Above: The first set to be painted and the first to run in passenger service was 672+682 on Good Friday, 18th April 2003. Pictured here at Cabin, the Line 2 orange and yellow set glide past bound for Little Bispham. Note the position of the Metro sticker on 682 which was latterly moved a few inches higher. (NM)

Progress TWIN·CAR
STARR GATE
via Sandcastle and Pleasure Beach

683

METRO
COASTLINES

673+683 were next and were outshopped in the Line 11 livery of turquoise and yellow. Unlike the first two, both cars retained their black and white destination blinds. The duo are seen just south of Broadwater on a Fleetwood to Starr Gate journey on Bank Holiday Sunday, 30th May 2004. (NM)

Taken literally six minutes after the photo opposite (but in sunshine), this is the fourth and most recently repainted set, 674+684 in the Line 4 deep purple and yellow livery. Although the double deck ban was lifted in April 2004, Twin cars are still used on Fleetwood service. (NM)

TRAMS & BUSES

Above: The operation of buses along the promenade hit a raw nerve in 2003 when Blackpool Transport introduced a service to Fleetwood in direct competition with their own tram service. Further to this the number of '111' tram replacement buses has also reached epidemic proportions over the last few years. In simpler days when the prom bus just ran to Gynn Square and was numbered '40', Routemaster bus 527 passes 'Auto Trader' advert car 678 at Talbot Square. (JB)

Opposite: One of those once in a lifetime moments as the Pontins advert tram passes the Pontins advert bus, taken from the pedestrian bridge by the Tower. Back in the days of '40' operation, the added attraction was of course the use of the ever popular 'Routemaster' buses. Today, the majority of prom buses are 20 year old Leyland Olympians and are used in one man operated mode. 707 is now a Millennium car. (JB)

1970's BRUSH CARS

Above: There were two single deckers in advert schemes in the 1970s, 622, on the cover, and this tram 634. It was outshopped in a special livery in April 1976 to mark the centenary of Blackpool Council. A year later the same tram was adopted to mark the Queen's Silver Jubilee with the addition of 'SILVER' and 'JUBILEE' advert boxes. In its 1977 pose, 634 passes Manchester Square for Starr Gate. Note the silver Tower top. (JB)

Opposite: Away from 622 and 634, the rest of the Brush car fleet carried the mundane and often weather-worn half green/half cream livery in the 1970s. Complete with trolley pole, roof advert boxes and Corporation crests, 631 approaches South Pier. The advert boxes encourage you to 'Rent-a-set' from Rumbelows and drink 'Wilson's Great Northern Bitter'. (JB)

1980's BRUSH CARS

Right: Into the 1980s and the all-over advert tram explosion. This is 633, 'The World's First Post Office' tram, but of course, it was the second! In the photo 633 is experiencing severe trolley trouble on the Pleasure Beach outer loop while the track is being relaid on the inner loop. 5th May 1984. (TW)

Left: Moving on seven years from the Silver Jubilee advert (page 22) here is 634 in what was its fourth all-over advert design. This one was a double sided affair with Blackpool Zoo on one cab and one side while the other cab and side (shown) had a pleasing yellow, grey, pink and blue effect for 'Splashland' at Derby Baths. 634 is seen outside depot in October 1984. (TW)

Right: Twenty years on and 633 and 634 are still doing the rounds. 634 remains an advert car while 633 has been completely rebuilt into the Illuminated Trawler. The pair pass at Talbot Square on Easter Sunday, 12th April 2004. (NM)

FROM THE MONORAIL

Even today the Monorail which skirts the Pleasure Beach affords fine views of the amusement park and seafront and this was certainly the case in this late 1960s photo which features Balloon car 724. The tram is typical of the era with a gold fleet number under the drivers cab window, side roof windows, trolley arch and trolley. The area around 724 has changed a great deal over the years and further building work will be completed in 2004. While 724 has been rebuilt and the Coronation car to the right has been scrapped, our old friend the Irish Sea, remains a never-changing feature of an ever-changing world. (JB)

Taken just a few seconds earlier than the photo opposite, the famous South Shore Open Air Baths can be viewed in all their glory. A victim of their age and design, the whole complex was razed to the ground in the mid 1980s to make way for The Sandcastle which still occupies the site today. Amongst the many pools within the complex was a 15ft deep pool with an array of diving boards to choose from, something which would be totally outlawed today. In the background is the South Pier while the Railcoach, complete with orange trolley tower, offloads at the 'polo' type tram stop. Judging by how empty the car park is, perhaps the Baths are closed, although back in the 1960s the motor car was certainly not the favoured mode of transport in the resort. (JB)

602 TAKES THE SPUR

On 12th October 2001, a private hire trip was booked for a filming sequence with comedienne Dawn French, for which 602 was selected. The tram was stabled on the outer loop at Pleasure Beach but the film crew were delayed and the loop was required for crew meal breaks. With the tram crew utilised elsewhere, 602 had to be moved, so the duty inspector opted to stable the tram on the rarely used spur track. (All NM)

1: 602 was driven in the wrong direction around the loop, trolley first.

2: The points were changed.

3: 602s trolley took the wrong wire and had to be moved.

28

4: The tram cautiously entered the spur.

5: The Inspector kept an eye on the trolley.

6: Car 710 had to wait for 602 to clear the points.

7: 602 is stabled while 636 passed on the main line.

BOAT CAR 603

In 1968 when the tram fleet was renumbered, Boat car 228 became 603 and ran for only six seasons with this number until 1975. The following year the tram was painted into a mainly white livery with blue, orange and grey stripes and exported to America for Philadelphia's bi-centennial celebrations. The car's bogies were regauged to 5ft 3in. 603 returned in 1978 and after a period of storage, returned to America in the early 1980s.

Above: On its way out of depot for a morning of specials, car 603 has its destination blinds changed. (TW)

Left: 603 as remembered in its final days in Blackpool, stored in Blundell Street depot on 22nd May 1982. The Trailer car behind the Boat is 688. (TW)

BOAT CAR 602

It may well be that cars 622 and 707 were the first true all-over advert cars in the 1970s and that 603 was the first Boat not in green and cream, but over the years a number of trams have carried distinctive short term advertising for special events or shows in Blackpool.

Above: 602 at Talbot Square about 1975 or 76. The tram advertises the International Motorshow special which took place between 22nd - 26th August. (TW)

Left: Happy Birthday! Spring Bank Holiday Monday 2004, and 602 and 604 pass at Tower. 70 years ago these two trams may well have passed at this location and other than modern windscreens and bright liveries, they are exactly the same. (NM)

YELLOW OMOS

Above: Out of the box, in mint condition and probably no more than a few weeks old, the delightful OMO 4 in sunshine yellow and crimson livery stands at Fleetwood Ferry. It's working route 3, according to the '3' in the windscreen and note the early form of ticket machine for the driver. To the right is a clock which would have told would-be passengers the time of the next ferry to Knott End. Sadly this fine tram car missed out on the 1985 celebrations having been withdrawn in March of that year. In January 1987 the car was broken up. (JB)

Left: The first one of all, OMO 1, leaves Talbot Square for Little Bispham in the summer season of 1974. By this time the OMOs had had a special timetable written for them which kept them on a loop to loop circuit but avoided Fleetwood in the day. (TW)

Right: The last of the 'plum and custard' cars was OMO 9 which came on stream prior to Christmas 1974. The tram is seen here at Talbot Square on 28th August 1975. The slow loading of the OMO cars often led to scenes like this where drivers would fill to capacity while a special was waiting behind. OMO 9 is one of a few cars which was still running as a Railcoach after OMO cars 1 to 5 had entered service. (TW)

CREAM OMOS

Above: From the spring of 1975 when OMO 10 was introduced, through until September 1976, the nine 'plum and custard' OMOs were painted into what became the standard livery for these cars - red and cream. Taken in 1977, a short while after the photo on page 22, OMO 3 passes a rather deserted Manchester Square on its way to Starr Gate. (JB)

Opposite: On the descent from Cabin to Gynn Square, OMO 13 glides past the cameraman on a morning journey to Starr Gate. Although it entered service in June 1976 with a pantograph, the photo here shows the car running with a trolley, although the two wooden pantograph supporting planks are still visible on top of the trolley tower. Car 13 ran for exactly eight years. (JB)

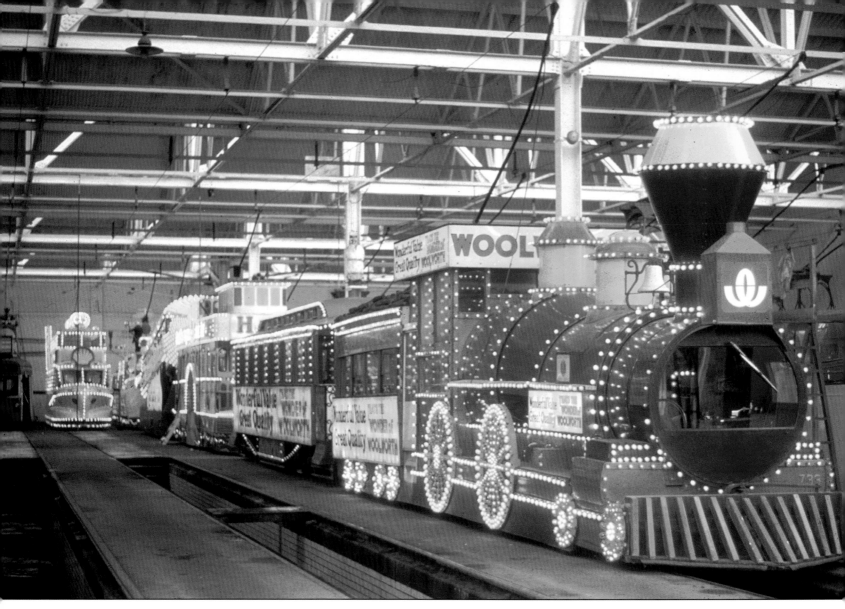

ILLUMINATED TRAMS

Above: Full house! A fantastic shot of Blackpool's former Illuminated fleet in depot, prior to evening service. Front right is The Western Train, 733+734, then The Blackpool Belle, 731, then 732, The Rocket and at the back, 736, HMS Blackpool. To the left is 735, The Hovertram. At the time this photo was taken, 731 was coming to the end of its working life and was withdrawn at the end of the 1978 Illuminations. The other five cars continued until 1999. (JB)

Opposite: Another priceless photo which oozes atmosphere. 731, The Blackpool Belle, eases its way around the curve from Hopton Road to Lytham Road for another evening of tour duty around 1968/69. Hawk-eyed readers will spot short sections of rail leading down Lytham Road to the front and left hand side of the tram. 731 was exported to America in March 1982. (JB)

DOUBLE DECKERS 2004

Right: The very first double deck tram to be painted into the Metro livery was 710. There is a bit of a debate as to what colour the tram actually is. Pink? Light purple? Dark pink? In this photo taken at Thornton Gate on a bright sunny day, the car is very much in the pink! (NM)

Left: 708 in the 1970s livery was another car withdrawn in early 2004. Luckily it was duly reinstated and one of its first duties was to tow a failed Millennium car from Fleetwood to depot on Sunday 30th May. 708+718 leave Ash Street. (NM)

Opposite: 724 is the latest Balloon to be rebuilt into a Millennium car and it entered service at Easter 2004. The tram, seen here at Thornton Gate on Thursday 27th May, is painted in the Line 5 livery. Compare this 724 to the other one on page 26. (NM)

CORONATION CARS

Above: The Channel 4 programme 'Salvage Squad' has recently dedicated two hour-long programmes to the restoration of Coronation car 304. The tram last ran in Blackpool in October 1970 and after 32 years of storage and on/off restoration attempts, it returned to Blackpool on 9th June 2002. Today it is fully restored to working order and painted in original livery. The photo above shows 304 in the early 1960s at Talbot Square. Note the cars to the right of the tram, parked up for the day! (JB)

Opposite: 643 was the fourth Coronation car to have its VAMBAC equipment removed in favour of the more traditional control system. This was short-lived for this particular tram as it was withdrawn from service only five years later. The photo shows 643 in its last summer of service, 1970, complete with roof advert boxes, an orange trolley tower and the drab half green/half cream livery. What a mighty fall from grace these cars suffered. (JB)

TRAM DEPOT

The tram depot at Rigby Road has always been an interesting point of call for all Blackpool tram enthusiasts. Built to house the modern Streamlined fleet of the 1930s, the building has remained more or less unchanged for the past 70 years, unlike the tram cars which have sheltered inside it.

Right: Railcoach 264 with rebuilt towing ends peeps out of road three in this March 1967 shot. Note the imposing depot doors. (TW)

Below: An interesting green/cream line up on roads two, three and four with 724, 637, 638 and 717. The one man operation experiments on 638 are remembered with the odd square shaped window behind the cab. (TW)

ON LOAN

Back in 1981 the idea of loaning trams for the 1985 Centenary Celebrations became reality when Bolton 66 arrived in the resort. 23 years and many trams later, the Vintage cars, as they are known, are now a regular sight on the promenade. A new practice, introduced in 2003, now means that three or four of these trams are used in passenger service every weekend between May and the end of the Illuminations, and with five particular cars of interest, a splash of real heritage tram car enhances the regular Blackpool fleet.

Above: Car 40 was built for the Fleetwood Tramroad in 1914 and spent many years running between Fleetwood and Blackpool North Station. In the photo the tram is having its trolley turned at Cabin on 30th May 2004. (NM)

Left: 513 originates from Sheffield and was built in 1950. Due to a severe derailment in May 2003, this tram (along with Stockport 5) is now banned from running north of Cabin, although in reality it only needs to run between Pleasure Beach and Cabin. Centenary car 642 passes 513 at Cabin on the same day. (NM)

722 DERAILMENT

Sand blowing from the beach and covering the tram rails is an ongoing problem in Blackpool and the danger of it became all too clear on 11th July 2001 when, on a late evening journey to depot, car 722 derailed and ended up on the adjacent road.

The top photo shows the tram in the aftermath of the incident. The sand patch in the foreground forced 722s front bogie off the rails and the tram veered across the road, blocking the entire northbound carriageway. The photo opposite shows 722 minus its front bogie on its way to depot for repair, towed by 929. (NM)

NO LIVERY BRUSH CARS

Right: Every once in a while a tram will appear in service without a livery! This is normally due to an old advert livery coming to the end of its contract and no new advert being available for painting. This is 622 or 'Casper' as it became known, in all white livery passing through Talbot Square in August 2001. (NM)

Left: One of the most striking 'no liveried' trams in recent years is this one on 627 - deep purple! Caught in the late evening sunshine, 627 looks quite menacing against an evil sky! The tram is at Pleasure Beach in October 2000. (NM)

STANDARD CARS

Above: A book on Blackpool's trams wouldn't be complete without a mention of the Standard cars, and following the return of Standard 147 from America, both residents and visitors can enjoy a ride along the prom on a Standard car once more. This photo shows Standard car 159 outside Marton depot. Note the swivel head trolley and the destination blinds of 'LAYTON'. (JB)

Opposite: In 1959 cars 158 and 159 were decked out as pseudo Illumination cars and in addition to their promenade duties, both trams undertook Illumination tours during the autumn. They served as a stop-gap between the original Illuminated fleet of the 'Gondola', 'Lifeboat' and 'Progress' cars which had been constructed between the wars and which by the late 1950s/early 1960s, were coming to the end of their days. These were superceded by the fleet on page 36, but for eight years between 1959 and 1966, 158 and 159 could be found at Talbot Square - as per the 1961 photo - awaiting their turn on tour duty. (JB)

WINTER HEAT

Things you never thought you'd see in a Blackpool tram book - a page dedicated to heaters! Both pointless and useless on a hot day in July but a vital part of any vehicle during the winter. Only two trams (627 and 679) now retain the type of heater that was fitted in the 1960s. Placed above the bulkhead in each saloon, the principle was simple: A filament would glow and a fan behind it would turn when the driver applied power notches, thus blowing waves of lovely heat into the saloon!

Above: Full internal view of 627s saloon, complete with heater unit over the bulkhead. (NM)

PLEASE STATE DESTINATION
AND TENDER CORRECT FARE
CHANGE FOR NOTES

Left: Close-up of the beast! Although simple in design and there is only one per half tram, it is surprising how much heat these units can generate on cold winter evenings when the saloon doors are only opened a dozen times on a full length journey. (NM)

ODDS & EVENS

Right: Time for a coffee? Well, why not enjoy it in the company of OMO 10 at the Wokefield Conference Centre near Reading! Upon withdrawal from service in November 1992, OMO 10 lingered on for a few more years before being purchased and transported to Reading in June 1996. The tram was painted into the local bus livery and retro-fitted as a seating area for visitors. (NM)

Left: Probably for the first time in a Blackpool tram book, a photo of the middle section of Twin car 676+686. This set is very much the odd one out as the other six still retain their disused centre destination boxes. It is not known when or why this pair had their boxes removed, but it's another strange quirk and another little bit of the history which makes the Blackpool tramway so unique. (NM)

Other titles available...

Opposite: An angel with a bow and arrow affixed to a lighting pole and three 70 year old British built tramcars below! Where else could this be but Blackpool! Blackpool Tower to be precise on Monday 31st May 2004, with 600 passing as a special for Pleasure Beach, 701 awaiting to take over from another tram for Starr Gate and 722 loading up for Cleveleys on a timetabled journey from Starr Gate. (NM)

Back cover: Another stunning shot from the Monorail, this time featuring a Railcoach, loading up on the outer loop. For many years this was the principal loading stop for passengers. Note the 'Polo' stop sign. The Railcoach has long gone but the Inspector's hut remains, although not in a coat of pink! Signs adjacent to the hut promote Illumination tours and advise passengers that it is 'This side for North Pier, Bispham and Fleetwood'. (JB)